Crabapples

LITTLE CATS

Bobbie Kalman & Tammy Everts

 Crabtree Publishing Company

www.crabtreebooks.com

Crabapples

created by bobbie kalman

for John and Mary George

Editor-in-Chief
Bobbie Kalman

Writing team
Bobbie Kalman
Tammy Everts

Managing editor
Lynda Hale

Editors
Petrina Gentile
Janine Schaub

Computer design
Lynda Hale
David Schimpky

Color separations and film
Dot 'n Line Image Inc.

Printer
Worzalla Publishing Company

Illustrations
Barb Bedell: pages 16-17, 22
Jeannette McNaughton: pages 10, 26

Photographs
Nancy Adams/Tom Stack & Associates: page 27 (bottom)
André Baude: page 18
Cincinnati Zoo: pages 25 (top), 26 (top)
Mary Clay/Tom Stack & Associates: page 28 (bottom)
Terry Farrell: page 19 (bottom)
Warren Garst/Tom Stack & Associates: page 24 (bottom)
James Kamstra: page 24 (top)
Thomas Kitchin/Tom Stack & Associates: front cover, pages 8, 9 (top), 10, 23
Joe McDonald/Tom Stack & Associates: page 25 (bottom)
Gary Milburn/Tom Stack & Associates: page 27 (top)
Motophoto Portrait Studios: page 19 (top)
Brian Parker/Tom Stack & Associates: pages 4, 21
Diane Payton Majumdar: pages 5 (top), 6, 11
Kevin Schafer/Tom Stack & Associates: page 28 (top)
Wendy Shattil & Bob Rozinski/Tom Stack & Associates: page 12
Dave Taylor: pages 5 (bottom), 15, 29
Dave Watts/Tom Stack & Associates: page 26 (bottom)
Michelle West: page 9 (bottom)
Robert Winslow/Tom Stack & Associates: back cover, title page, pages 7, 9 (left), 13, 14, 20, 22

Special thanks to
Terry Farrell, Jackie and Ron Pfander, Alma and Ken Shindler, and Michelle West for their photos of purebred cats; also to John Becker at the International Society for Endangered Cats for his kind assistance.

Crabtree Publishing Company

PMB 16A
350 Fifth Ave,
Suite 3308
N.Y., NY 10118

612 Welland Ave.,
St. Catharines,
Ontario, Canada
L2M 5V6

73 Lime Walk
Headington,
Oxford OX3 7AD
United Kingdom

Cataloging in Publication Data
Kalman, Bobbie, 1947-
    Little cats

(Crabapples)
Includes index.

ISBN 0-86505-611-0 (library bound)   ISBN 0-86505-711-7 (pbk.)
This book examines various species of little cats, with attention to their appearance, behavior, habitat, and breeding.

1. Felidae - Juvenile literature. I. Everts, Tammy, 1970- .
II. Title. III. Series: Kalman, Bobbie, 1947- . Crabapples.

QL737.C23K35 1994   j599.74'428   LC 94-5314
                                                                    CIP

WHAT IS IN THIS BOOK?

LITTLE CATS

Some cats are little. Some cats are big.
Little cats are smaller and lighter than
big cats. The lynx below is a little cat.

Big cats and little cats are different in other ways as well.

- All big cats are wild, but some little cats are tame.

- Most big cats can roar, but little cats cannot. Little cats meow or make loud yowling noises instead!

- Cats wash themselves by licking their fur. This is called **grooming**. Little cats, such as the caracal below, groom themselves more than big cats do.

CATS ARE MAMMALS

Cats are **mammals**. Mammals are animals that have hair or fur. A female mammal carries her babies inside her body until they are born. Newborn mammals drink milk from their mother's body.

CAT FEATURES

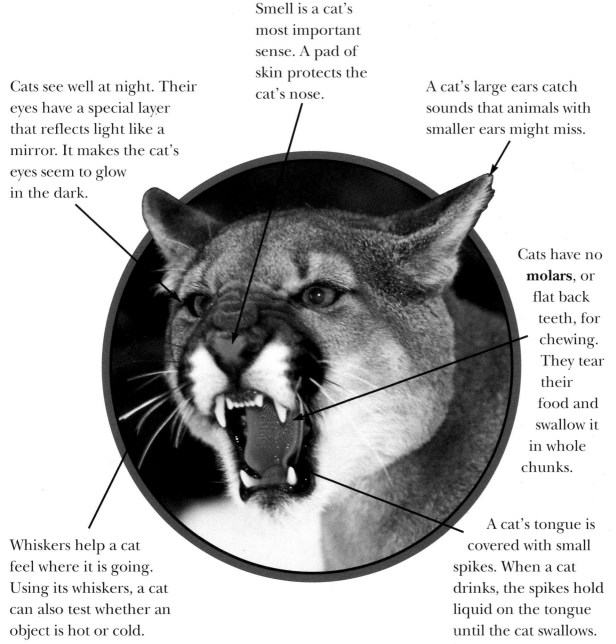

Smell is a cat's most important sense. A pad of skin protects the cat's nose.

Cats see well at night. Their eyes have a special layer that reflects light like a mirror. It makes the cat's eyes seem to glow in the dark.

A cat's large ears catch sounds that animals with smaller ears might miss.

Cats have no **molars**, or flat back teeth, for chewing. They tear their food and swallow it in whole chunks.

Whiskers help a cat feel where it is going. Using its whiskers, a cat can also test whether an object is hot or cold.

A cat's tongue is covered with small spikes. When a cat drinks, the spikes hold liquid on the tongue until the cat swallows.

CAT HOMES

Little cats live in almost every part of the world.

Some little cats live on grassy plains. Some live in nests. Some live in trees.

Some little cats live in hidden caves. Some live in snowy mountain forests.

Some little cats live in houses and barns. Does a little cat live with you?

LITTLE CAT FOOD

Cats are **carnivores**. Carnivores eat only meat. Cats are hunters. Most cats hunt at dusk and sleep during the day. Wild cats kill and eat small animals. Mice, rats, birds, and insects are part of their diet. Some pet cats hunt as well, but most are fed cat food.

Cats sometimes eat grass. Perhaps it helps them digest their food. A plant called catnip drives cats crazy! They love to smell and eat catnip!

Some pet owners feed their cats vegetables, ice cream, and even cake! Too much of this kind of food is not good for cats. Kittens and cats love milk, but milk is not a healthy drink for adult cats.

CAMOUFLAGE

A cat needs to hide from its prey when it hunts. **Camouflage** is a color, shape, or pattern that helps animals hide. Spotted cats blend into the sun-spotted forest floor. Striped cats can hide in trees and tall grass. Brown or gray cats blend in with rocks, trees, or desert sand.

BABY CATS

Mother cats have from one to five babies at a time. Some mother cats have six babies or more! Baby cats are called **kittens** or **cubs**.

Kittens are born blind. Their eyes do not open for a week or two. Kittens are born without teeth. They get their baby teeth, or **milk teeth**, when they are three or four weeks old.

Mother cats feed and protect their kittens. The cougar mother on the next page guards her cub. Most father cats leave before the babies are born. Male bobcats are the only father cats that help care for their young.

bobcat kitten

THE CAT FAMILY TREE

The cat family tree is divided into big cats and little cats. Not all cats fit into these groups. The cheetah is in a family of its own, close to the big cats. The cougar is in its own family, close to the little cats. There are only four kinds of big cats, but there are many kinds of little cats. We could not show them all.

Big Cats

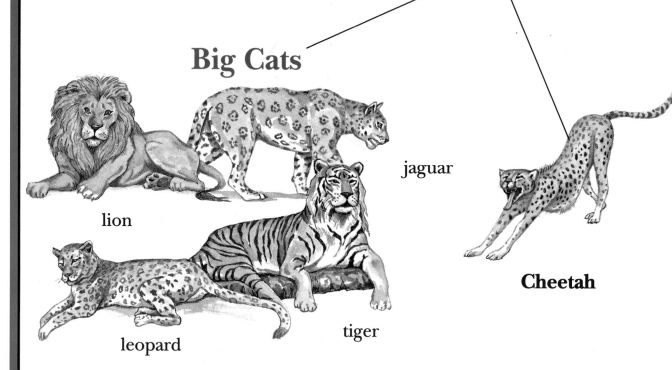

lion

jaguar

leopard

tiger

Cheetah

The **miacid** was a small carnivore that lived 40 million years ago. It is the ancestor of modern meat-eating animals such as cats, dogs, and bears.

Cougar

Little Cats

Pet cats

Wild cats

jaguarundi   ocelot   margay   manul

lynx

bobcat   caracal

wildcat   fishing cat   serval

CAT FRIENDS

Pet cats make great friends. They come in all shapes, sizes, and colors. Some cats have long, silky fur. Other cats have fur that is short and sleek. A few cats have no fur at all!

The cat in the top picture is a Maine coon cat. Coon cats are the biggest of all pet cats. They have fluffy striped tails that look like the tails of raccoons.

Manx kittens are born without tails. Which three small wild cats have very short tails? Use the index and find them in this book.

Tabby cats are the most common housecats. They are striped cats that come in different colors. The girl on the opposite page thinks her tabbies are wonderful pets!

COUGAR

Cougars look like big cats, but they are not. Instead of roaring, they let out loud yowls that sound like human screams. Cougars are skilled hunters. They hunt small animals.

Cougars are also known as **pumas** and
mountain lions. They live in deserts,
forests, and snowy mountain areas.

LYNX AND BOBCAT

The lynx and bobcat belong to the same family. Both have short bobbed tails and large, furry feet. Their wide feet are like snowshoes. They keep the lynx or bobcat from sinking when it walks on snow.

The lynx on this page lives in a northern forest. Snowshoe rabbits are its favorite food. The bobcat kitten on the opposite page lives in a cave. It will grow up to hunt rabbits, birds, and small deer.

MARGAY AND OCELOT

Margays and ocelots are small, shy wild cats. They live in hot, wet forests called **rain forests**. They hunt mice, lizards, frogs, and birds. An ocelot uses its teeth and claws to pluck the feathers from a bird before eating it! Margays and ocelots climb well. This margay is carefully approaching an anteater.

Margays and ocelots look almost the same, but the ocelot is larger and has a longer tail. Its face is thinner, and its eyes and ears are smaller. Some people have tried to tame young ocelots, but the kittens soon become wild again.

FISHING CAT

The Asian fishing cat is twice as large as a regular housecat. It has webbed front paws that make it an excellent swimmer. The fishing cat eats fish, clams, and frogs. It even hunts goats!

WILDCAT

Forest wildcats are tiny. They look like pet tabbies, but they would not make good pets. They do not like people. They do not even like other cats! Wildcats live in thick forests and high up on mountains, far away from people.

MANUL

The manul lives in deserts and mountain areas. It is the size of a housecat. It has long, silky fur and a furry ruff around its neck. The fur on its stomach is extra long and thick to keep the cat warm when it sleeps on cold ground. The manul makes unusual sounds. It can bark like a dog or hoot like an owl!

SERVAL

The serval is a fast, graceful cat. It has a long neck, small head, and very long legs. Its tail is short. The serval lives in hot grassland areas. Some servals are black, but most are orange-yellow with a pattern of spots and stripes.

JAGUARUNDI

The jaguarundi has "jaguar" in its name, but it is not a jaguar. Jaguars are large, spotted cats. The jaguarundi is much smaller and has no spots. The jaguarundi lives in tropical forests. It is an excellent swimmer and tree climber.

CARACAL

The caracal is also called the **desert lynx**. It is a fierce-looking cat that lives on hot, dry deserts and plains.

A caracal's short hair helps this cat stay cool. The long tufts of black fur that sprout from its ears help the caracal feel objects in its way.

The caracal's long legs and sleek body allow it to run and hunt well. Caracals hunt small antelopes, hares, and birds. Sometimes a caracal stands on its back legs when it is eating and holds its food in its front paws.

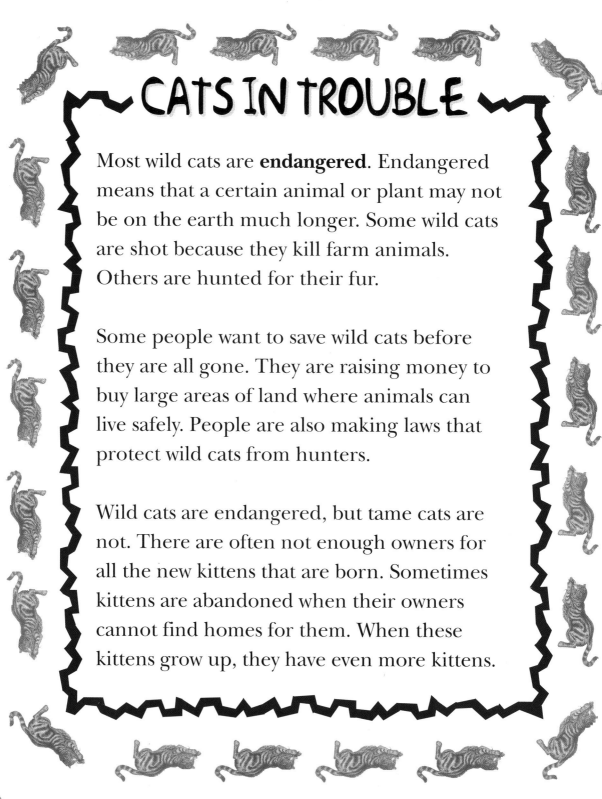

CATS IN TROUBLE

Most wild cats are **endangered**. Endangered means that a certain animal or plant may not be on the earth much longer. Some wild cats are shot because they kill farm animals. Others are hunted for their fur.

Some people want to save wild cats before they are all gone. They are raising money to buy large areas of land where animals can live safely. People are also making laws that protect wild cats from hunters.

Wild cats are endangered, but tame cats are not. There are often not enough owners for all the new kittens that are born. Sometimes kittens are abandoned when their owners cannot find homes for them. When these kittens grow up, they have even more kittens.

WORDS TO KNOW

ancestor Something from which something or someone is descended

camouflage Patterns or colors that blend into the environment

carnivore An animal that eats only meat

endangered Describing a species that is in danger of dying out

groom To wash fur by licking it

mammal A class of warm-blooded animals with backbones and fur or hair

milk teeth The first or baby teeth of a young mammal

molars The flat teeth at the back of the jaw used for chewing

plain An area of level land

rain forest A hot forest that receives a lot of rain

ruff The hair around the neck of an animal

tuft A cluster of hair or feathers

INDEX

WHAT IS IN THE PICTURE?

Here is some more information about the photographs in this book.

page:	
front and back covers	Bobcats live throughout North America, except for the far north.
title page	Bobcats are most active at dawn, dusk, and night.
4	Lynxes can be found in North America, Europe, and Asia.
5 (top)	Pet cats love to climb trees but often have difficulty getting back down!
5 (bottom)	Grooming not only keeps fur clean, it helps the cat stay cool.
6	Female cats stop nursing their young after two months.
7	Cougars live in North, Central, and South America.
8	This lynx kitten is just two weeks old.
9 (left)	In the winter, cougars leave the mountains to follow deer and other prey.
9 (top right)	This six-week-old lynx kitten has just begun to explore the world outside its den.
9 (bottom right)	Abyssinian cats have been kept as pets for thousands of years.
10	A cougar kitten has a spotted coat until it is six months old.
11	Milk helps kittens grow.
12	Ocelots live in the rain forests of Central and South America.
13, 14	Bobcat kittens stay with their mother for six to nine months.
15	A cougar kitten will stay with its mother for up to two years.

page:	
18	Tabby cats got their name from a Chinese fabric called "attabi," which resembles their fur.
19 (top)	Some people believe that Maine coon cats were brought to North America by Vikings.
19 (bottom)	The Manx cat has front legs that are shorter than its back legs, giving it a hopping walk.
20, 21	Some cougars are as big as leopards; others are just a little larger than pet cats.
22	Lynxes roam vast areas of forest in search of food.
23	Bobcat kittens open their eyes one week after birth.
24 (top)	Margays have unusually large eyes and ears
24 (bottom)	Margays live in the rain forests of Central and South America.
25 (top and bottom)	Ocelots spend more time on the ground than margays do.
26 (top)	The Asian fishing cat lives in the forests of Asia.
26 (bottom)	Wildcats live in the forests of Europe.
27 (top)	The manul lives in the deserts and mountains of Asia.
27 (bottom)	Servals live in Africa.
28 (top and bottom)	Jaguarundis can be found from the southern United States to South America.
29	Caracals live in Africa and southwestern parts of Asia.

5 6 7 8 9 0 Printed in USA 3 2